Colours in Nature

Yellow

Lisa Bruce

Heinemann
LIBRARY

www.heinemann.co.uk/library
Visit our website to find out more information about **Heinemann Library** books.

To order:
☎ Phone 44 (0) 1865 888066
🖹 Send a fax to 44 (0) 1865 314091
💻 Visit the Heinemann Bookshop at www.heinemann.co.uk/library to browse our catalogue and order online.

First published in Great Britain by Heinemann Library, Halley Court, Jordan Hill, Oxford OX2 8EJ, part of Harcourt Education.
Heinemann is a registered trademark of Harcourt Education Ltd.

Editorial: Jilly Attwood and Claire Throp
Design: Jo Hinton-Malivoire and bigtop, Bicester, UK
Models made by: Jo Brooker
Picture Research: Catherine Bevan
Production: Séverine Ribierre

Originated by Dot Gradations
Printed and bound in China by South China Printing Company

ISBN 0 431 17233 1 (hardback)
07 06 05 04 03
10 9 8 7 6 5 4 3 2 1

ISBN 0 431 17238 2 (paperback)
07 06 05 04 03
10 9 8 7 6 5 4 3 2 1

British Library Cataloguing in Publication Data
Bruce, Lisa
Yellow – (Colours in nature)
535.6
A full catalogue record for this book is available from the British Library.

Acknowledgements
The publishers would like to thank the following for permission to reproduce photographs:
Ardea p. **15** (Dennis Avon); Bruce Coleman pp. **13** (Hans Reinhard), **16** (Kim Taylor), **19** (Rosemary Calvert); Corbis pp. **6-7**, **22**, **23**; Digital Vision p. **10**; Imagestate p. **11**; Max Gibbs p. **12**; Photodisc p. **14**; Robert Harding p. **8**; SPL pp. **4-5** (David Nunuk), **9** (Tony Buxton), **17** (Favre, Jerrican), **18** (Alan L Detrick), **20** bottom right (Agestock/Joel Glenn), **20** top left (Agestock/Ed Young), **21** bottom right (Th Foto-Werbung), **21** top left (Agestock/Ed Young)

Cover photograph reproduced with permission of Max Gibbs

The publishers would like to thank Annie Davy for her assistance in the preparation of this book.

Every effort has been made to contact copyright holders of any material reproduced in this book. Any omissions will be rectified in subsequent printings if notice is given to the publishers.

Contents

3

Yellow in nature

Nature is full of wonderful colours.

What can you think of in nature that is yellow?

Yellow Sun

High in the sky the
Sun shines with a
bright yellow light.

These bright yellow sunflowers turn their heads to face the Sun.

Yellow sand

Beaches

Desert

Sand can be yellow.
Where can you find sand?

Yellow animals

Roar

The lion's coat and mane are yellow.

This cat has many shades
of yellow in her fur.

Purr!

Yellow fish

This fish is bright yellow.

13

Yellow birds

When chicks hatch, their feathers are **soft** and **fluffy**.

The cockatoo raises its yellow crest
when it is frightened.

Squawk!

Yellow insects

A bee has yellow and black stripes on its body.

BUZZ

BUZZ

The colours are a
warning to other animals.

What do bees make?

Honey

Yellow flowers

Spring flowers are often yellow.

Daffodils

Tulips

Do you know the names of these flowers?

Yellow food

Peppers

Lemons

Sweetcorn

Which of these do you like to eat?

Pineapples

Changing colour

When bananas first grow they are green.

In the sunshine they ripen to become yellow.

Index

The end

Notes for adults

This series supports young children's knowledge and understanding of the world around them. The four books will help to form the foundation for later work in science and geography. The following Early Learning Goals are relevant to this series:
• begin to differentiate colours
• explore what happens when they mix colours
• find out about and identify some features of living things, objects and events they observe
• look closely at similarities, differences, patterns and change
• ask questions about why things happen and how things work
• observe, find out about and identify features in the places they live and the natural world
• find out about their environment, and talk about those features they like and dislike.

The Colours in Nature series introduces children to colours and their different shades by exploring features of the natural world. It will also help children to think more about living things and life processes, which may lead on to discussion of environmental issues. The children should be encouraged to be aware of the weather and seasonal changes and how these affect the place in which they live.

This book will help children extend their vocabulary, as they will hear new words such as sunflowers, cockatoo, crest, daffodils, tulips, insects, peppers, lemons, sweetcorn, pineapples and ripen.

Additional information

The stems of sunflowers turn so the flowers can always face the sun. Sunflowers are farmed for food as well as beauty. Sunflower seeds contain large amounts of vitamins. They can be eaten as a snack, or used to produce oil for cooking and making into margarine. The Lesser sulphur-crested cockatoo (page 15) lives in the islands of Indonesia. The male has a white plumage with bright yellow ear-covers and crest feathers. The female is almost identical, but generally smaller.

Follow-up activities

Using paper plates and cutting paper petals create sunflowers. These can be attached to canes of various heights to show stages of growth. Measure the children against the sunflowers.

The children could also sing nursery rhymes with a yellow theme such as 'Twinkle, twinkle little star,' and 'Daffodowndilly'.